Chakras

How To Boost Your Energy And Psychic Abilities. Open Your Mind Power To Fight Depression And Anxiety

(The Simple Manual For Understanding Chakra Function And How To Use It In Daily Life)

CutbertoGasca

TABLE OF CONTENT

What Are the Chakras 2

An Overview of the Seven Primary Chakras in Their Most Basic Form.. 6

THE META-STATE'S CONSCIOUSNESS OF ITSELF 12

The Muladhara Chakra, which is sometimes referred to as the First Chakra 20

The Manipura Chakra, which is also known as the Solar Plexus Chakra, is the third chakra. 30

Reestablishing the connection between the Root Chakra and the Earth...36

It is the job of the Solar Plexus Chakra to help you cultivate your own personal power and inner strength...51

Bring Back the Sense of Harmony to Your Heart Chakra..60

Get rid of the energy that's been accumulating in your throat chakra. 66

Intuition and information are processed through the Third Eye Chakra, also known as the Knowledge Center. 81

How the Throat Chakra Contributes to Effective Verbal and Nonverbal Communication 88

CHAKRA REIKI MEDITATION for the Purpose of Healing. 100

Understanding the Role of Sensuality in the Process of Spiritual Development and Awakening the Erotic Self 104

Meditation Is Necessary Before Healing the Chakras 119

Techniques for Correct Pronunciation as Well as Chanting 132

Using Chakras to Manifest Your Desires and Improve Your Relationships 135

Aromatherapy as a Means of Restoring Chakra Balance 150

Asanas for Restoring Harmony to the Heart Chakra in Yoga 153

"Ajna" The area known as the Third Eye The Chakra is located in the middle of the forehead. 159

Bringing the Chakras into Harmony Through Complementary and Alternative Healing Methods and Other Practices 167

Instructions to Help You Get Started Practicing Belly Breathing 176

What Are the Chakras

The body contains a number of energy centers known as chakras. If the physical body has organs that are vital to survival, then the spiritual body, also known as the energy body, will have chakras. It is essential to maintain the health of your chakras because having unhealthy chakras would result in having poor physical health. According to the findings of a study, infirmities of the physical body first make their appearance on the energy or spiritual body before making their way into the physical form. Additionally, the chakras are the entry and exit points for energy in and out of the body. In order to activate the Kundalini, you must first ensure that your chakras are robust and in good health.

Because of the connection that exists between the energy body and the physical body, you need to make sure that your chakras are clear of debris and in good health. The chakras, particularly the primary chakras, are what make it possible for energy to move freely throughout the body. When a person is sick, it is highly likely that one or more of his chakras are affected in some way by the illness.

It is important to keep in mind that the chakras do not merely relate to your physical body; rather, they have the potential to influence your life. For instance, if you have a healthy root chakra, it indicates that you have a level of stability in your life. If your heart chakra is strong, there is a good chance that love and harmony are abundant in your life. If your heart chakra is weak, however, these qualities may be lacking. As you can see, the condition of your chakras and how well they are functioning can have a significant impact on the course of your life.

The development of one's chakras is another method for acquiring psychic power. Consequently, developing your chakras should be an essential component of your practice from now on. It is important to note that there are seven primary chakras located throughout the body. These seven chakras can be found along the spine, beginning at the bottom of the spine and progressing all the way up to the crown chakra, which is situated a few centimeters above the top of the head. Let's go through each of them one at a time.

8. The Crucial Role of the Root Chakra

The entire physical body, including the bones, muscles, blood, and other internal organs, receive their energy from the root chakra. It controls the body temperature as well as the growth rate of infants and children. It is the hub of one's own efforts to survive or preserve themselves.

The root chakra is helpful in the treatment of a wide variety of illnesses, including cancer, leukemia, low vitality, allergy, asthma, sexual ailments, growth problems, and psychological issues.

Many thanks and best wishes!! Upon starting out on this path toward a more prosperous and healthy life through Prosperity Healing. You will take a significant step forward in the direction of liberating your true potential for abundance and prosperity if you read this ebook and make an effort to comprehend its contents, which include principles, practices, and techniques. Always keep in mind that you have the ability to design a life for yourself that is characterized by financial independence, fulfillment, and joy. Get ready to reawaken the energy of prosperity that lies dormant within you so that you can manifest the life you so justly deserve.

As a Pranic Healer who specializes in Prosperity Healing, I am able to offer assistance to individuals by assisting them in recognizing and transforming their energetic patterns and beliefs related to abundance. This gives them the ability to attract and create greater financial prosperity in their own lives.

An Overview of the Seven Primary Chakras in Their Most Basic Form

The root chakra, which is the first of the major chakras in your body, may be found at the bottom of your spine. Its name comes from its location. Because of its "earthly divine" quality, it continues to be accessible even after one's connection to the planet is strengthened. The harmonious functioning of one's root chakra leads to the development of a person who is robust, self-assured, and powerful. This chakra is symbolized by the colors brown, black, and different hues of red, especially earthy and warm reds. It is located in the center of the chest. As a color symbol, the color red is most widely used to represent the root chakra. The root chakra is located at the base of the spine. Imagine that the ground is red while you concentrate on the chakra, and as you do so, deeply root yourself from the base of your spine all the way down to the nourishing depths of the soil. This will help you connect with your spirituality. Imagine that this earth energy begins its journey at the base of your spine, makes its way down through your legs and into your feet, and then continues its journey below the surface of the world. The Muladhara chakra, also known as the root chakra, is an indication of your dependency on the energies of the ground to cleanse and heal you. This dependence is a manifestation of your connection to the earth.

Imagine the Tibetan monks who, while meditating, sit on top of mountains with their legs crossed and their feet firmly planted on the earth. Because of the way that they sit, they have a very strong connection to the ground below them. The root chakra extends far beyond the bounds of the body, all the way into the bowels of the earth. The root chakra is the location of the energy known as kundalini, which resembles a serpent and is the conduit via which prana goes up and down the spine. The root chakra is located at the base of the spine. Due to the fact that it is widely acknowledged as the most potent type of life-giving feminine energy, it will bestow upon you a great number of spiritual gifts. The energy that can be drawn from the root chakra as a result of this is boosted. You can increase the breadth of your consciousness by reawakening the power that resides dormant at the base of your spine and giving it the name kundalini. As a result, gaining a solid foothold in Muladhara is as effective as the color red, which stands for power, confidence, strength, and accomplishment in addition to being a symbol of beauty. In addition to this, you will experience an unending wellspring of joy and vitality in your body.

There is nothing more humbling and healing than being anchored in the present moment and being determined to enhance your appreciation for your spiritual abilities and what life is giving you with at this very time. Being anchored in the present moment also helps you appreciate what life is giving you with at this very moment. Spending time connecting with the earth and becoming grounded is a good approach for maintaining your connection to the prana that runs throughout the cosmos. Since the earth is our natural habitat, spending time connecting with the earth is a wonderful method. As a consequence of this, the Muladhara chakra will become more developed. You should have the tenacity of a mountain, the freedom of a bird, and the ability to root yourself deeply and widely in the earth like a tree does. Whenever you find yourself feeling doubtful or fearful, connect yourself to the flow of the strong and intense crimson energy that comes from the Muladhara chakra. While you do this, see it emerging from your soles while you mentally repeat the word "lam." Consider putting a red stone around your neck, particularly if you are having substantial issues that can be linked to fear, and ground yourself on a daily basis by going for a walk or sitting out in nature with the purpose of profoundly anchoring yourself. Also, ground yourself by going for a walk or sitting out in nature with the intention of profoundly rooting yourself.

THE META-STATE'S CONSCIOUSNESS OF ITSELF

When we make an effort to enter a meditative state, the very first step that we need to take is to enter a meta-conscious state. The implication of this is that we should be aware of the fact that we are thinking at all times. And that we are not these thoughts ourselves, but rather that we are observing them from "outside" of ourselves as though we were looking in on ourselves from the outside. This process is also known as the "observer" getting older, which is another name for it. Does it seem to be simple? It is. To a certain degree. And yet, we are all guilty of becoming lost in our own thoughts from time to time, aren't we?

It's possible that you're wondering how all of this connects to what I've talked about in prior chapters of this book in terms of being in the flow state. "Being at one with our actions and thoughts" and everything else that goes along with it. "Being at one with our actions and thoughts" There will be a rise in the number of instances in which such seeming inconsistencies occur.

We, as human beings, are not a singular entity; rather, we are composed of a number of processes that function relatively independently of one another. These processes make up who we are as a species.

To put it another way, think about it from this point of view: Relationships are the building blocks of a life.

acontinuous connection with oneself, with other people, and with the environment that one is immersed in at all times. There are two distinct halves to the world that we inhabit. Without another person to act as a counterpart or partner in our perception, it is impossible for us to perceive anything.

Through the cultivation of our meta-awareness, we are able to arrive at the experiential realization that our existence is not a unitary entity, but rather is composed of a range of distinct processes that are, for the most part, independent from one another. This is something that can only be known through direct experience. Considered to be one of these processes is the thinking process. As we have seen, this process is referred to as manas in the yoga philosophical tradition.

In a purely pragmatic sense, we require meta-awareness as a key prerequisite in order to detect when our mind starts to wander during the course of a meditation session.

WORKSHOP TO INCREASE META-AWARENESS THROUGH CHAMBER 7 EXERCISES Investigation and Research

Stand up straight and press your eyes tight. Become aware of your breathing without striving to modify it. Now, think of "in" when you inhale (as long as it takes naturally, don't force it), and think of "one" when you exhale. Take a big breath "in" and then let out "two"

And so on up until the hour of ten.

After then, begin once more at the number one. It's probable that you'll experience a sense of resistance from your thoughts when you try to concentrate on one item.

Maintain your focus on your breath at all times, even when new thoughts enter into your head; pay them as little attention as you can when they do.

When you become aware that you have been following a train of thoughts for a time and have lost track of the number of repetitions, bring yourself back to the exercise in a kind and patient manner and begin counting from one again.

Continue doing this for approximately five minutes. Use a timer to keep track of how long you spend meditating, and try to find an area where you won't be disturbed for at least a few seconds.

So, how did everything turn out? During that length of time, your thoughts most certainly drifted a few times, which is completely typical. There is no difficulty with doing that at all.

In this specific exercise, the most critical thing is not to be able to retain our focus on a single item — in this case, the experience of breathing — but rather to detect when our attention has wandered and then to actively bring it back. It's akin to working out with weights. You won't develop the kind of strength you need for day-to-day tasks if all you do is use it to hold them if that's all you do. This demands for a switch in load priorities. And quickness.And the ability to adapt.

At this point, you have certainly come to the conclusion that sitting down for periods of meditation can be a problem, at least in the beginning.

For the first several years after I first started practising formal meditation, the sensation of exertion was the one that stuck out to me the most as being associated with the technique. During the course of my formal practise, there were countless occasions on which I did not find myself approaching what I would define as a contemplative level of consciousness at any point.

It was just this process, repeated over and over again: my thoughts would wander, I would ultimately become aware of them, and then I would bring my mind back to the task at hand.

Interestingly, after doing this every day for a few weeks, the meditative state began to occur on its own at some point during the day. I must add that at that time I was also regularly attending at least three one-hour group meditations of various traditions each week, in addition to my yoga courses, which at that time all featured lengthier meditations and breath awareness.

For instance, if I were walking somewhere, I could pause for a few seconds to listen to the birds singing in a tree by the side of the road, and all of a sudden, there would be an unbelievable clarity that seemed to connect my senses with what they were hearing. However, during the many years that I spent practising formal meditation, this practically never occurred to me.

The Muladhara Chakra, which is sometimes referred to as the First Chakra

This chakra, which can also be referred to as the lotus with four petals, can be found quite close to the base of the spine. The anus and either the testicles or the cervix are brought into contact with it. The ultimate happiness, the bliss that comes from inside, the bliss that comes from connection, and the bliss that comes from having bravery and power are all represented by the various petals of this lotus flower. It is possible to credit the joyous nature of her petals to her because it is believed that she is a reflection of the head chakra on the physical level. This principle of creation, known as Brahman, is at the root of all that exists in the cosmos, and its nature is identical to that of this particular chakra. We are able to make the assumption that it just maintains the physical shape of the body and that it hides both the history of its origins and the possibility for further human evolution. This is something that we are able to do because of the evidence that we have.

Because of this, the health and well-being of the body are dependent on it continuing to work regularly in order for it to be protected. This is the body's foundation and support system. The characteristic of scent, the color orange-red, and the element of the earth are all connected to this chakra. Its symbol, which is an elephant with a black stripe around its neck, is meant to represent worldly qualities such as power, steadfastness, steadiness, and support. The yellow square that is inscribed within the center of the mandala or yantra that portrays this chakra serves as a visual representation of the terrestrial attributes that are associated with this chakra. In addition to this, it has a triangle on its surface that represents the will, the knowledge, and the action. This triangle is known as the Tripura, and it is located on its surface.

In addition to the bones, skin, muscles, and nerves, as well as the hair, Muladhara has an effect on the genital region, as well as the genitalia, the kidneys, and the accumulation of sperm. It has been connected to a variety of physiological diseases, such as hemorrhoids, constipation, sciatica, and issues relating to the prostate, among others. It is linked to a person's sense of smell, and the vibration it generates is what causes the lungs to either expand or contract, depending on the state of the person's sense of smell.

Mishra suggests in his writings that practicing pratyahara, which is a distraction of the senses, on this chakra is the best way to achieve mastery over wrath, lust, and greed. Pratyahara means "withdrawal" in Sanskrit. An imbalance in them is believed to be the cause of a number of symptoms, including longing and despair, among other things.

By meditating on this chakra, a person can achieve mastery over a variety of bad emotions, including attachments to luxury and falsehoods, pride, envy, and narcissism, among others. Pandit explains that the Muladhara is the area of the body that is in charge of regulating both conscious and unconscious actions and impulses. A blazing triangle with the color of blood that inflates the kandarpaVayu may be found in the yantra, which is the symbolic representation of the chakra. This Vayu is the origin of sexual excitement, which is vital to the survival of the human species as a whole. According to what Motoyama stated, when this chakra awakens, it unleashes suppressed emotions explosively, causing a person to suffer acute irritation and psychological instability, along with a violation of normal sleep patterns and excitability. This can also cause a person to have a disruption in normal sleep patterns.

It is believed that one of their crimes can be cleansed through meditation on the deity linked with this chakra, Mahadeva, who is said to sit with his face turned away from the practitioner. Brahma, the god of absolute creative power, presented this chakra to the goddess Dakini Shakti as a gift. The term "Dakini Shakti" refers to the creative force behind all that exists. By meditating on this chakra, reciting the mul mantra in a devotional state of mind, maintaining mental serenity, and concentrating on this chakra, you will be able to reawaken her goddess. The energy known as Kundalini is said to be coiled up in a manner that has three and a half times as many twists as this chakra, in accordance with the cosmology of yoga. The SushumnaNadi, also known as the "Nadi that carries the stream of life," the VajraNadi, also known as the "Nadi that carries the electric stream," and the Brahma Nadi, also known as the "sound stream" or the "stream of spirit," are all thought to merge at this particular point. Yogis hold a firm belief that this is the location.

Alexandrite is a noun.

The mineral chrysoberyl comes in many different variations, and one of them is called alexandrite. It is most well-known for its ability to change color, which causes it to appear green in areas with higher light levels and red in conditions with lower light levels. This color difference can be traced directly back to the presence of chromium in the sample. Because chromium is able to absorb light of varying wavelengths, its color might appear to shift depending on both the light it is exposed to and the angle at which it is viewed. The alexandrite precious stone is one that is not only fascinating but also quite hard to come by.

There are also synthetic kinds of Alexandrite that were made in laboratories; these types of Alexandrite have no spiritual meaning and are completely devoid of any distinguishing qualities. It is believed that the natural form of alexandrite can stimulate one's intuition, enthusiasm, and creativity, as well as bring about prosperity and wealth. In addition to this, it helps to restore a healthy balance to the neurological system, which in turn contributes to an improvement in one's mental clarity, attention, and emotional equilibrium.

It is stated that exposing oneself to the stone known as Alexandrite will encourage personal development and change on a spiritual level. It is considered that it can be of assistance in the process of encouraging spiritual growth and consciousness. It is conceivable that doing so could allow a person access to more advanced levels of awareness and knowledge than they have previously possessed. due it can assist in opening the heart to new experiences and opportunities, alexandrite is sometimes associated with the heart chakra. This is due of the stone's potential to help open the heart.

AUTHENTIC PROPERTY

Depending on the angle from which it is viewed and the amount of light to which it is subjected, color Alexandrite can give the impression of being either green or purple.

Because of the great level of hardness it possesses, alexandrite is a gemstone that is both durable and long-lasting. Because it has a Mohs hardness value of 8.5, which makes it among the most challenging gemstones to cut and polish, it is not very common.

In most cases, alexandrite will have a clarity that is somewhere between transparent and translucent, and it will have a vitreous sheen.

The spiritual benefits of alexandrite include a boost to one's intuition and creativity, as well as an increase in one's chances of experiencing joy and success in life. In addition to this, it is said to promote mental clarity and attention while at the same time providing harmony to the neurological system.

There are many distinct varieties of gemstones, including but not limited to the following forms of Alexandrite: pulled Alexandrite, Alexandrite grown in Czochralski, Alexandrite formed in hydrothermal environments, and Alexandrite generated in a flux.

Alexandrite is an exceptionally unique gemstone that can only be found in a limited number of locations all over the world. Countries such as Russia, Sri Lanka, Brazil, Madagascar, and Tanzania are examples of some of these locations.

The Manipura Chakra, which is also known as the Solar Plexus Chakra, is the third chakra.

Your third energy wheel, which is associated with the element of fire, may be found approximately four fingers higher up on your torso than your belly button. This location can be found on the left side of your body. The interpretation of this chakra's name in English is one of my favorites. Because mani means "shining gem" and pura means "place," you can conceive of your Solar Plexus as the location of the gem that shines. This is because mani means "shining gem" and pura means "place."

The solar plexus chakra is where the energy known as samanaprana can be found stored. The digesting process, which is also the means by which we take in nutrients, requires a certain amount of energy, which can be obtained from the sun as well as from foods that contain heat. It is the source of the warmth and light that you sense, comparable to how you may feel after spending some time outside in the fresh air on a day when the sun was shining brightly. In addition to this, it is associated with our intelligence, ego, willpower, and even, on rare occasions, our aggressive impulses. When you take into consideration the power of fire, this makes complete sense. It is absolutely necessary to cultivate this chakra via regular practice in order to achieve general equilibrium in both the body and the mind.

This chakra is represented by a triangle that is nestled inside of a lotus flower and serves as its symbol. Each of the 10 petals of the lotus flower represents a debilitating trait that we have to conquer in order to restore the chakra's state of equilibrium. The following characteristics best describe them:

Lack of knowledge on the spiritual realm

Fear

Jealousy is a serious moral flaw.

Putsch or "Coup d'etat"

The disgrace

Desire to eat Conviction of guilt

Illusion of truth

The absurdity of allowing oneself to be overcome with melancholy

According to one interpretation, the inverted triangle with its point facing downward in the middle of the lotus flower is meant to symbolize fire.

How to Tell If Energy Is Not Moving Through Your Solar Plexus Chakra and What It Means for You

Indigestion, heartburn, ulcers, and even weight gain can all be caused by insufficient activity in the solar plexus chakra. This can also lead to a number of other digestive difficulties. It's possible to struggle emotionally with low self-esteem and a lack of faith in yourself when you don't believe in yourself. This can occasionally result in "analysis paralysis," which is when a person thinks too much to the point that they are unable to take any action. Because of this, your motivation will suffer because you won't be able to get anything done. This will have a knock-on effect on your motivation. When this chakra is blocked, digestion troubles become more severe, which can potentially lead to issues with the pancreas, liver, and/or colon as well as food disorders and diabetes. When the flow of energy isn't working properly, it can be difficult for some people to take responsibility because they have an attitude of being a victim. It's possible that an unhealthy fixation with suppressing angry outbursts is at play here. It is also possible to say that this is the case when the solar plexus chakra is overactive while at the same time there is a greater need to be right and competitive. People that partake in an excessive amount of activity in this field face the danger of developing traits such as hyperactivity, egotism, and a lack of openness to new ideas. For some people, taking sedatives to control their hyperactivity could seem like a reasonable and appealing option.

Those who are self-assured and have a crystal-clear grasp of both who they are and their goal in life are likely to have a solar plexus chakra that is in a state of equilibrium. Those who have a crystal-clear understanding of both who they are and their mission in life are likely to have a balanced solar plexus chakra.

They are determined to achieve their objectives and possess the perseverance necessary to do so. Because of this, individuals are in a position to make more sound choices and are in the right frame of mind to recognize when it is suitable to engage in risk-taking behaviors. They are able to effectively digest the food that they eat, which contributes to their robust metabolism and abundant supply of energy as a result of the fact that their digestive system functions as it should.

Reestablishing the connection between the Root Chakra and the Earth

1. The root chakra holds a tremendous amount of potential for rooting oneself in the earth, which can be accessed through meditation. Right now, while you are finding a position that is comfortable for you and concentrating on your breathing, you should spare a few moments to direct your attention to the root chakra. Imagine that there is a red light all around you, and as you do so, give yourself permission to feel protected, safe, and secure. Imagine that there is a red light all around you. This is a brand new realization that was just brought to light. Throughout the length of the meditation you are performing for the root chakra, make sure that you keep

as much of this light's presence with you as you possibly can.

Step 2 At this point, as we start this meditation, you should focus on bringing the energy of your breath all the way down into the center of your root chakra. This will assist you in reestablishing a connection with your earthly roots. Because your consciousness is already at that level, you should find it somewhat easy to have the impression that your breath can also make its way down there. This is because your consciousness is already at that level. Visualize yourself being able to send out roots from this root chakra, just like a tree does, while keeping your breathing pattern relaxed and regular. Do this while you continue to focus on the sensation of being grounded. When you are trying to unwind and take some slow, deep breaths in the here and now, try to picture yourself as a tree.

Visualization will assist you in gaining your bearings.

Step 3: With your eyes closed, begin by sending those roots downward from your root chakra, and then sit in that serene silence. After you've done that, repeat the process. Imagine that any thoughts, emotions, or feelings that may enter your head in the future are breezes that pass through the towering branches of the tree that you are. This will help you to better understand how your mind works. You will be better equipped to handle any situation that arises as a result of this. Imagine if at this time of year your branches do not have any leaves on them; the winter must have been exceedingly harsh. You are aware that spring will arrive sooner rather than later, yet despite this fact, you are ready to take on everything that the remaining months of winter might throw at you because you are excited for spring to arrive.

4. Observe how those thoughts are transported via the branches of your mind in one way, and then how they are completely transported through those branches and emerge on the opposite side of your mind. Whatever it is that comes from within you will eventually come to pass since it is only as powerful as a breeze. This is because it is only as powerful as it appears. Allow any distractions to come and go, but this time, regard them as though they were a light rain that might be falling from the sky. This will help you stay focused. You are not worried despite the fact that you can feel the pattern of drops pushing against your bark since such distractions are easy to come and go. This is because distractions like this are easy to move on

from. Because you are the most robust tree in the woods, there is no reason for you to be concerned about anything that may, in the long term, contribute to your progression toward maturity.

Step 5 Give yourself permission to let those thoughts and ideas that are distracting you come and go as readily as the wind and the rain as you focus on establishing your center. As you dig your roots deeper into the soil, you'll gradually gain a better understanding of the new environment in which you are now residing. Imagine that you are confident, strong, and extremely knowledgeable. Take a deep breath in and allow yourself to be filled with the love and sustenance that the world has to offer you as you slowly and deliberately exhale. Completely let out your breath, and then, using the grounding wires that are sprouting from your root chakra, send your own unique love back down to the earth.

Step 6: In this new reality, which is characterized by connectedness and groundedness, inhale deeply and direct your attention toward enhancing your strength. When you root with the land, you take in the nutrients that are in the soil and you experience the love that the earth has for you. Both of these things are changed into your own, freshly established strength. Imagine that you have been whisked back in time to that tree and are able to observe the buds emerging on the tree's branches. Soon, the top branches of your mind will be green with lush growth, and shortly after that, you will discover that this grounding effort is bringing your ideas to levels that are beyond any degree that you could have conceived of.

Step 7 As you breathe into your root chakra and feel confidently connected to the soil, strive to speed up time around you. This will help you ground yourself in the present now. This will assist you in establishing a deeper connection with the here and now. Observe how the passage of time leads to the development of branches that are entirely green as well as an increase in height of a few centimeters. Observe how the winter season gradually gives way to the arrival of spring, which brings with it the blossoming of flowers and the maturation of fruit into seeds that can be planted later. After you've established your grounding, you should think about the foundation that will be built for you. Now that summer is getting closer, you will start to see fresh blossoms and fruit forming on your branches as they are being established in their new growth. This will continue until the summer. During the fall, you will observe those formerly green branches turning orange, then red, and ultimately brown before they eventually wilt and fall to the ground. This process continues until the branches die off completely.

Step 8 Your mind, your spirit, and your physical body are all interwoven components of a tree that you grow with the changing of the seasons by obtaining new knowledge on how to develop and which seeds you will finally disperse on the ground. You do this by cultivating your mind, spirit, and body through learning new information on how to develop and which seeds you will eventually scatter on the ground. You have the ability, with each breath you take, to increase your sense of possibility while also enabling the anchoring thread of your roots to become more solid through the power of your purpose. You have a crystal clear picture in your head of the kind of growth you want to see. Now, construct that environment outside of meditation, but bring the information that you received as a tree – that you pull from the root chakra within you – with you everywhere you go. You can do this by imagining that you are pulling it out of the center of your body. Perform this action so that you will never be without access to it.

Good morning, and thank you for joining me for this calming meditation on the heart chakra. Permit me to take you through the steps involved in opening and balancing the fourth Chakra, which is the Chakra that connects you to the energy of love. Find a cozy place where you can easily shut out the world around you, and make sure you're seated in a position that is both comfortable and relaxed at the same time. Inhale without agitation while maintaining a calm and steady pace, and then exhale without agitation. You are free to close your eyes whenever you feel inspired to do so while you are meditating on the chakras and focusing your complete concentration on each one in turn. Because of this, you are able to more effectively bring the chakras into equilibrium. You eventually come to the realization that the events that take place in your life are symbolic, and that there are important life lessons to be gleaned from them. First, take a gigantic gulp of air, and then gently and thoroughly let it out of your system.

Completely relax each inhale as well as each exhale. You do this over and over again, taking a breath in and then releasing it. Take a moment to notice how a wave of serenity is currently washing over your entire body at this precise moment. You will be able to connect with the love that is already a part of you if you direct all of your consciousness to the very center of your chest. At this time, you should focus your attention on the heart chakra, which can be found in the exact center of your powerful chest. This chakra is colored with a verdant green that is reminiscent of the color of nature. Consider it as having the shape of a star with six equal sides as one way to think about it.

Embedded with aesthetically pleasing designs at every turn. In the exact middle of your chest, it emits a piercingly brilliant light that resembles a sage-like green. Imagine that you are able to shift this Chakra simply by thinking about it, and that you have complete control over it. Observe how it picks up the pace while preserving its bright green color right up until the point where it most likely can't move any faster than it is already going. It is recommended that this mantra be recited five times. I made the decision to be loving. I made the decision to be loving. I made the decision to be loving. I made the decision to be loving. I made the decision to be loving. Become aware of your breathing as you take a few slow, deep breaths and visualize the heart chakra shining brightly. Do this while you take the deep breaths. It will swell up and become considerably larger, spreading outside from your body in all different directions as it does so. Having the privilege of experiencing the power of genuine love at its deepest possible level right now. How would you describe the feeling that you experience when you are in the heart chakra? I'd like to hear your thoughts on this. When you do this, you are opening your heart and allowing the love that is held within you to spread throughout the entirety of the planet. Your love is a bottomless pit of force that cannot be exhausted. It emerges in a never-ending stream from the deepest parts of your being to the outside world. The feeling of being loved without conditions is analogous to having someone tenderly massage your entire chest area. It is abundantly seen that the heart chakra is entirely open, and its movement is not hindered in any way. It's almost as though you can feel the radiance of lime and green spinning around it. Good. Take a deep breath in and as you do so, visualize yourself bringing energy from the heavens and the ground into the center of your chest. Continue doing this for a few more breaths. Carry on in this manner for a couple more complete breaths.

Your entire body is bathed in unconditional love, which gently illuminates each of the other chakras and bestows upon them the ability to move and open through the transformational power of love. As a result, your entire body is saturated with love. You are listening to the words, and there is not the slightest bit of wrongdoing in my heart. Good. The hard chakra is now completely open, and it is prepared to link the love that is already existing within you with the love that is already in the world. The love that is already present within you can now be linked with the love that is already present in the world. astonishment at the fact that you are able to do so. bringing back and reigniting an interest or enthusiasm that had been dormant for a long time. directing your focus once more inward, towards your heart and your thoughts. Again, make sure to take some nice, deep breaths. Just one more time, inhale deeply as you exhale. The inhalation and the exhale are equally pleasant experiences. Bring your focus softly back to the here and now where it belongs. Feel the love that's been building up in your heart expanding into your chest. While you are breathing, open your eyes and try to think about the events that have happened to you in your life from a new point of view. More intricately intertwined with the idea of love than at any other time in history.

It is the job of the Solar Plexus Chakra to help you cultivate your own personal power and inner strength.

The Solar Plexus Chakra, also known as the Manipura Chakra, is the third energy center in the chakra system. It is also sometimes referred to as the Sacral Chakra. The Solar Plexus Chakra can be found in the top part of the abdomen, in the region that is adjacent to the diaphragm. It is linked to our sense of personal power, as well as our self-esteem, confidence, and inner fortitude. In the following chapter, we shall delve into the profound qualities that are associated with the Solar Plexus Chakra. We will cultivate an awareness of its purpose in our life, a greater grasp of its emotional and energetic parts, the ability to recognize symptoms of imbalance, as well as powerful practices for healing and balancing this transformative energy center.

Having an Awareness of the Importance That the Solar Plexus Chakra Plays in Regards to One's Personal Power:

The brilliant shade of yellow that is linked to the Solar Plexus Chakra is meant to be interpreted as a symbol of the transformative energy that is kept inside this chakra. It is the center from which all of our own strength, willpower, and self-assurance radiate outward into the world. The Solar Plexus Chakra bestows upon us the capacity to have self-assurance in who we are, to set reasonable boundaries for ourselves, and to conduct ourselves in a manner that is harmonious with our authentic selves. Because of this energy center, we are able to generate a robust sense of self-worth and gain access to our inner strength, which in turn enables us to make use of the power that is already within us.

To Have a Better Understanding of How the Solar Plexus Chakra Affects Our Emotions and Our Energy State Feelings, ideas, and our overall levels of energy are all influenced by the Solar Plexus Chakra. This chakra is located in the solar plexus. Our sense of personal identity, as well as our self-esteem and self-confidence, are both under its direct control. When the Solar Plexus Chakra is in a condition of balance, we are able to experience sensations of self-empowerment, motivation, and the capacity to successfully fulfill our goals. It enables us to take on problems, establish ourselves with grace and clarity, and project a sense of personal strength all at the same time. On the other hand, indications of an unbalanced Solar Plexus Chakra can include poor self-esteem, self-doubt, indecisiveness, or an obsessive drive for control. These are all symptoms of the third chakra, the sacral chakra. These symptoms can manifest themselves as a lack of faith in one's own abilities.

The following are examples of indications that indicate an imbalance or blockage in the Solar Plexus Chakra:

In the body, an imbalance in the Solar Plexus Chakra or a barrier in its energy flow can manifest in a wide variety of various ways, depending on the severity of the problem. In terms of an individual's emotional state, an imbalance in the Solar Plexus Chakra may result in feelings of insecurity, fear of rejection, a lack of motivation, or difficulty making decisions. Additionally, this may cause the individual to have difficulty digesting food. In addition to this, it may result in a behavior that is dominating or controlling, as well as an inability to accept personal responsibility for one's own acts. Some of the physical symptoms that may be induced by an imbalance in the Solar Plexus Chakra include digestive difficulties, stomach ulcers, or stress in the abdominal region. These can all be very uncomfortable conditions.

The beginning of the Kundalini awakening

This chapter is geared toward readers who have reached a point in their spiritual development where they are ready to begin direct practice aimed at kundalini awakening. In the next pages, you will learn 29 methods that can help you in accelerating the awakening of your kundalini, and the final half of the book will give you with 6 additional methods that you can try out to make your experience even better. Regardless of whether you had prior experience with the kundalini awakening or are just learning about it for the first time through this book, the guidance that is offered in this chapter is likely to bring substance, depth, and understanding into your experiences as you continue on your journey.

Techniques for the Awakening of Consciousness

You will be able to advance beyond a simple knowledge of kundalini and awakening with the help of the possibilities that are offered in this section. You will then be in a position where the information can be put into practice. These alternatives range from meditation techniques to recommendations on how to interact with others and simple strategies for navigating the world; all of them will assist you in navigating the world. Put out your yoga mat, light some incense, and clear your mind so that you'll be ready for the following increase in difficulty.

You should try to incorporate some of the kundalini yoga practices into your routine.

Adding physical layers to your spiritual practice will be highly beneficial to you to the extent that you are able to do it. You will reap greater benefits according to the extent to which you are able to carry out the action. When it comes to the awakening of the kundalini in particular, as opposed to general awareness or the balancing of the chakras, Kundalini yoga is the practice that is best suited to get started with. This is especially the case if you are not only interested in achieving general awareness or balancing your chakras. With the support of kundalini yoga, you will be able to go past those chakra obstacles. This practice will also assist you in getting the kundalini moving and enhancing your contemplative practice within the context of the moving human body. You will be astounded at how well everything fits together when you first begin to complement your practice with yoga, and this feeling will continue for as long as you continue to do so.

The level of Shakti that is active within a person can be raised by making use of their gaze.

Visualization is one of the most significant methods you may use to enhance the flow of shakti, which is also known as your kundalini, throughout your entire body. This flow of energy is crucial for many spiritual practices. The ancient Indians were on the right track when they gave human-like names to the cosmic wells of energy that are housed within each and every one of us. They were aware of the powerful function that metaphor and imagery can play in illuminating the workings of the interior body as well as the subtle energy that a person carries, and they used these tools accordingly. As an illustration, the word "kundalini" derives from the Sanskrit phrase "little coiled one," and it may either refer to the serpent that encircles the universe or the source energy (shakti) that is located at the base of each of our spines. The mental picture we are meant to conjure up is of a snake becoming enchanted as it twists its way through each of our chakras. The things that we are expected to envision in our brains include a lot of different things, and this is one of them. It will be of increasing benefit to your practice if you are able to incorporate visualization into it more frequently.

Bring Back the Sense of Harmony to Your Heart Chakra

The heart chakra, also known as the Anahata chakra, is the fourth of the seven chakras and is located at the center of the chest. Its name pretty much tells away its position, which is in the middle of the spine, close to where the heart would be. The word "anahata" in Sanskrit can be translated into English as "unhurt," "unbeaten," and "unstruck," respectively. Your heart chakra, which is also called the sacral chakra, is where you keep the memories of the truths that are the most challenging for you to express. This chakra is connected to the element of air, which is very apt considering its function. Just like love, the air is all around us and even inside of us, and we are able to feel it even when our eyes are closed. This is because the air is all around us and even inside of us. Your energy can be compared to air that is flowing freely through you when the heart chakra has been cleansed and energized. This occurs when the heart chakra is open. The energy of the heart chakra, which is associated with love as well as the process of transformation, is represented by the color green. Green is also the color that represents nature. The words "I love" are used as the mantra for the Anahata, which is depicted as a six-pointed green star nestled inside of a flower that has 12 petals.

It is time for you to close your eyes at this point. Investigate whatever it is that you are going through at this very moment and make an effort to get a feel for it. Are you terrified at this moment? Have you ever been diagnosed with anxiety? Do you have the feeling that you are loved by others? Are you experiencing a joyful mood right now? If you have noticed that you are getting more preoccupied by negative emotions, it is possible that your anahata chakra is congested and in need of some maintenance. Rarely do individuals have the capacity to simultaneously experience the feelings of love, hatred, and fear. The majority of the time, one of these emotions predominates over the experience, while the other two remain in the background. It's possible that you'll continue to experience these sentiments even when they are in the background, but the intensity of those feelings won't compare to the intensity of the emotions that are in control. It is possible for a person to feel irrational emotions such as fear and contempt, for instance, even while they are completely in love with another person. Love, on the other hand, has a tendency to take a back seat when someone has been through a challenging breakup or a heartbreak because fear or hatred have a tendency to take center stage until the individual has fully recovered and is ready to give their heart again.

The growth of the heart chakra often does not start until a person is in their early 20s or later, when they begin to engage in more serious romantic relationships. This is because the heart chakra is associated with love and compassion. On average, it appears between the ages of 21 and 28. This is the age range in which it occurs most commonly. Around this time, many people have their first experience with real and genuine love, and they also discover the courage to put themselves out there, despite the danger of suffering a broken heart or being turned down.

A wide range of things that occur in our day-to-day lives have the potential to have an effect on the heart chakra. Because of this, you have a responsibility to pay attention to it and make sure that it is not blocked in any way at any time. Once you have achieved a level of balance in your heart chakra, you will be able to feel a wide range of positive feelings, including happiness, joy, and love that is not conditional on anything. These feelings have the potential to teach you to enjoy life in novel and more effective ways.

When your heart chakra is closed, you may discover that it is difficult for you to love yourself, to feel joy, or to trust people. On the other hand, when it is open, you may discover that you are more optimistic, trustworthy, or joyous. It is general information that our mental and emotional well-being, in addition to our physical health, are significantly influenced by our emotions. This is also true for our physical health. When you are unable to exercise control over your feelings, you may find that you are overcome with feelings of anxiety, tension, and even sadness. These negative emotions have the capacity to strip away more positive ones, like as love and joy, from a person's life. At this time, it will be vital for you to work on the repair of your heart chakra.

You probably weren't aware of this, but the Earth also has its very own heart chakra, weren't you? Between Shaftesbury and Glastonbury in England's southwestern region is where you'll find the closest thing to an Anahata that you'll find anywhere in the globe. The mysterious and alluring Stonehenge monument, which is situated only a few miles away, contributes to the allure of this site.

Get rid of the energy that's been accumulating in your throat chakra.

Because it is the fifth chakra in your energetic system, the neck chakra, also known as the fifth chakra, is of utmost significance to both your mental and physical welfare. This is due to the role that it plays as the fifth chakra. This chakra is also known by its Sanskrit name, Vishuddha, which translates literally to "extremely pure." This is another name for this chakra. There is a clear connection between this chakra and the unadulterated nature of the air element, which may be inferred from the chakra's name as well as the color blue's association with it. Because of its location, the Vishuddha is commonly characterized as a pocket of air that is clear blue or white and sits in the back of the throat, close to the wall of the muscles in the neck and the spine. This is due to the fact that the Vishuddha is located close to the wall of the muscles in the neck and the spine.

If there is a blockage in your throat chakra, it will give out signals that are not overt but will let you know that something is wrong with your body. These are indicators that you should never ignore, and you should get to the bottom of the issue as soon as possible. It goes without saying that the moment you become aware of them, you shouldn't throw yourself into a state of fear. It only suggests that you ought to correct them at this time so that they don't cause any additional damage in the future.

By reading this chapter, you will gain an understanding of the ways in which your health and happiness are impacted when the function of the Vishuddha chakra is balanced, as well as the ways in which you may feel when this chakra is out of balance. You will be given an easy yoga routine to follow in order to clear your throat chakra and decrease the symptoms of the fallout that can occur when this energy center becomes blocked. The goal of this practice is to help you communicate more effectively with others. Because the opening of this chakra is more gradual than the opening of other chakras, you will also be faced with the symptoms that you may anticipate experiencing as the energy begins to flow through. This is due to the fact that the opening of this chakra is more gradual than the opening of other chakras.

The Many Parts and Responsibilities Played by Vishuddha

Your energetic system is not complete without the vishuddha, one of its most essential components. It is your obligation to provide you with the skills necessary for good communication, both internally and verbally. This includes providing you with the ability to effectively communicate with others. It is through the throat chakra that your thoughts and feelings are brought into sync with your speech. This enables you to convey whatever it is that is stored inside them in a manner that is more harmonious. In addition to this, it gives you a creative outlet for the thoughts and feelings that you simply are unable to convey through honest conversation. This can be in the form of writing, drawing, or performing an art form. Because the sacral chakra is where you receive your creative ideas, the health of this lower energetic center is directly related to your ability to communicate who you are and what you have to say. This is because the sacral chakra is the source of your creative ideas. In addition, this seems to imply that one of the most essential functions of the Vishuddha chakra is to work in conjunction with the other chakras.

The act of creating something new teaches you to recognize and value the things that have happened in the past as well as the unique skills that God has bestowed upon you. When you take stock of all the various abilities you possess, it is easy to realize that other individuals also have their own original ideas and skills to offer the world. This is something that everyone has to offer the world. You are motivated to pay more attention to the people around you as a result of the energy that is flowing through your Vishuddha chakra, which enables you to develop connections that are healthier for both parties involved.

You can reawaken the energy of your life by engaging in the practices of yoga and mindfulness and allowing that energy to flow freely via your throat chakra, which will have an impact on the physical functions of that chakra. When you enhance your capacity for self-expression, you offer your mind a chance to relax and become less crowded. When you do this, the benefits of increased self-expression are immediate. Because of this, the quality of your sleep will improve, you will have more energy for the activities of daily living, and the health of your body will improve overall.

Your throat chakra exerts influence over the organs in your body that are responsible for performing significant functions. One of these is the thyroid, which is an endocrine gland that regulates a wide range of processes, such as growth, immunity, cognitive functions, and the functioning of other endocrine organs. It is responsible for the operation of other endocrine organs. One more of Vishuddha's responsibilities is to ensure the proper operation of your respiratory system. Because of the muscles, blood vessels, and other forms of tissue that are found naturally in these locations, your neck and mouth are also able to absorb energy. This is owing to the fact that these areas are naturally there.

The chakras are not separate powers that are capable of enacting their own will on their own. However, it is imperative that we take a step back and emphasize that the most significant feature of chakras is the way in which they are connected to one another and how they flow throughout the body. This is because the individual significance of the chakras has been discussed to some extent up to this point in the book. One of the most important aspects of how these energy centers operate within the body is an individual's capacity to totally combine and connect all of their chakras with one another. We have made the discovery that the nadi behaves in this manner, which we found to be the case. You must initially think of your chakras as a single integrated system if you want to have a complete understanding of both the energy that flows through them and the chakras themselves. It is impossible to repair one problem without first addressing the problems that exist with the others. You can think of the components that make up your chakra systems as being similar to the components that make up a meal. Have you ever been in the position where you had all of the necessary ingredients for a dish, and they were all of a high quality, but you mixed them together in the wrong order, and the recipe was a complete and utter bust as a result? This is the way that you should think about chakras in order to put everything into perspective. Even if you balance or unblock each one of them individually, the only way that you will be able to truly cure them is by thinking of them as a single, interconnected system that needs to be kept in a condition of equilibrium. This is the only way that you will be able to truly cure them. In this chapter, we will discuss the ways in which the chakra system understands itself to be a harmonious and balanced system.

What Exactly Are the Categories of the Chakra System?

The first issue that needs to be addressed is the question of just what chakra systems are and how they operate. How do the different sections of the body, which are all located in such distinct locations, communicate with one another? In any event, the discussion that we had in Chapter 2 regarding the origins of chakras in Hinduism will serve as the jumping-off point for our investigation into the chakra system. This school of thinking proposes that the chakras are not discrete portions of your body at all, but rather a network of various sites throughout your body that permit energy to flow through them. One way to think of this system is as a multistory office building, with the spine acting as the elevator that connects each floor of the structure to the next. In addition to the building's foundation, the structure's lower floors are home to essential components such as electrical systems, sanitary facilities, and power generators. These floors also contain the building itself. When you go to the middle floors of the building, there is where you will discover the departments of administration and communication. These departments are responsible for overseeing the operations of the organization as well as maintaining its ties to the outside world. Executives, members of creative teams, and the chief executive officer all have offices on the upper levels of the building. All of these individuals are in charge of the most important aspects of the company, such as determining the path that the business will take in the future and thinking up creative solutions that will help the organization reach new heights of success. As you can see, each of these domains functions on its own. Despite this, they all have clear links with one another and a progression that goes from the highest level to the lowest one. If you place a disproportionate amount of emphasis on your lower floors, which are also referred to as your lower chakras, then you will never be able to obtain more superior knowledge or foresight. On the other hand, if you disregard these core chakras, which are also referred to as the essential functions of the organization, the remainder of the structure would suffer as a direct consequence. This comparison illustrates how the flow of energy through the chakras is critical to the chakras' capacity to carry out their roles on a spiritual level. The use of meditation and yoga as instruments to assist in the circulation of this energy, particularly in the direction of its ascent from the base chakra to the crown chakra, is crucial to the practice of chakras as well as the notion of chakras.

a Typical Example of Your Workout Routine

A great number of people get pumped up about the possibility of working out and the wonderful impacts it will have on them as a result of the activity. They picture themselves running in races of various distances. They are thinking about taking part in a challenge that involves doing push-ups. However, the vast majority of these people do not have enough time in their schedules to engage in physical activity. The defense that they just do not have enough time is the one that is used the most frequently.

Participation in Active Pursuits and Effective Time Management

People who claim they don't have the time to exercise either don't have the motivation to exercise or think there are other things that are more important than their health. There are two types of individuals that claim they do not have the time to engage in physical activity.

If you are serious about making this adjustment, you can't just sit about and hope that you will eventually find the time to start an exercise regimen. You are going to have to MAKE TIME for it in your schedule.

You might want to think about approaching your workouts in the same way that you approach the other elements of your life that are important to you. You put going to the birthday celebration of your child at the top of your to-do list, and you make every effort to ensure that you can make it. You will make an appointment to see a doctor if there is something that is upsetting you, and you will go in prepared. You organize your day-to-day activities so that you can attend a meeting with an important client.

Exercise should be a priority for you, so put it on your to-do list. Include some form of physical activity in your daily routine so that you may take advantage of the plethora of health benefits, both physiological and mental, that come along with regular exercise.

In order to exercise regularly, one must first master the art of time management. This is an absolute prerequisite. If you put a high enough priority on maintaining your physical health, you will find the time to exercise no matter how packed your agenda is. In place of one of the less important activities, you should engage in some form of physical activity. Because getting some exercise should be one of your top priorities, you'll need to approach this assignment with some inventiveness and flexibility.

Intuition and information are processed through the Third Eye Chakra, also known as the Knowledge Center.

Do you ever get the feeling that the same day is just repeating itself over and over again? It's possible that you were going about your day when all of a sudden you had the clear sensation that you had seen or been a part of this exact scenario previously. This could have happened while you were doing something completely different. Or, it's possible that you've encountered situations in which you had a gut feeling about what to do or how to respond, despite the fact that you didn't have any genuine context for the incident to base your decision on. It is true that regardless of how logical or sensible we may consider ourselves to be, many of us have had moments in which we were in touch with our inner knowing and intuition. The vast majority of us, as we progress through life, eventually cultivate an awareness of things that are not physically apparent or plain to us. We have the option of ignoring something, or we may choose to concentrate on it instead.

If we do not have an accurate grasp of these skills, we face the danger of missing out on opportunities to enrich our lives by making use of them. However, we may avoid this risk by gaining an accurate understanding of them. It is also conceivable for us to fall prey to the fallacy that such abilities are only possessed by a very limited set of people, which is not the truth. This is not the case, but it is nevertheless possible for us to fall prey to this fallacy. It will take some time and work on our part to correctly align our third eye chakra, but we won't be able to get there until we have a firm understanding of the concept behind it in the first place. The discussion in the next chapter will center on the third eye chakra and the role that it plays in each of our individual lives.

What exactly is the third eye chakra, and how does it function in the body?

The subtle body is the location of the sixth chakra, an energy center that can be found there. It is also the final chakra that may be actively worked on by devoting oneself to a spiritual practice on a day-to-day basis. This will allow one to bring their spirituality to a higher level. The "physical" locations of these chakras can give us with insight into the role they play in our spiritual development. This is true despite the fact that these chakras do not actually exist within the physical body. The third eye is situated in the human skull exactly in the middle of the forehead, precisely four inches behind the point where the eyebrows meet. This area of the head is known as the sphenoid gyrus. This chakra is shown as a pair of lotus petals with an inverted triangle positioned in the center of the pair of petals. There is a school of thought that holds that the inverted triangle is a symbol of enlightenment. A representation of the bija (seed) mantra that is often referred to as Om can be found in the middle of the symbol (this will be discussed in further detail later).

The color that stands for the human body's third eye chakra (also known as the brow chakra).

Indigo is the color that is said to represent the ajna chakra, which is also referred to as the third eye chakra. Specifically in relation to this chakra, what does the color blue signify? This is due to the fact that indigo is considered to be a particularly spiritual color in a variety of religions all over the world. In general, it is considered to be a color that assists in elevating our consciousness of ourselves as well as the environment that surrounds us. By utilizing it in this manner, we are able to expand our awareness and access a variety of alternate states of being that are not often accessible to us. This is another reason why people usually identify the practice of meditation with the color blue.

Indigo is a color that represents not just loyalty but also impartiality and fairness. To put it another way, this color tends to assist us in viewing things more accurately, rather than as we would prefer them to be. In a manner analogous to the second chakra, the third eye chakra heightens one's powers of perception and intuition. Additionally, the color is connected to the concepts of knowledge and intelligence.

Indigo can also be understood as a combination of the colors red and blue, both of which carry a great deal of weight in religious and philosophical contexts. Indigo is a color that is considered to be a happy medium between the agitation that is associated with the color red and the calmness that is associated with the color blue. Therefore, not only does this color signify vitality and vigor, but it also represents calmness and serenity. It is difficult to gain an understanding of our inner nature if we are unable to find peace and quiet.

Indigo is a color that is connected with transitions, both from life to death and from one realm of existence to another. This is not the least of its associations. This is significant because when our third eye chakra is aligned, we are able to perceive things that exist on a plane of reality that is beyond this one. This color is also taken into consideration to be a symbol of "escaping the material plane."

How the Throat Chakra Contributes to Effective Verbal and Nonverbal Communication

The functioning of the throat chakra, also known as the fifth chakra, is critically important to one's capacity to communicate with other individuals in a way that is both effective and crystal clear. There is a school of thinking that holds that this energy center is responsible for determining our capacity to articulate our thoughts and feelings in a way that is unequivocal and certain. This energy center is connected to the throat, the neck, and the mouth all at the same time. In this article, we are going to talk about the role that the throat chakra plays in communication, as well as the ways in which keeping a healthy and balanced throat chakra can help us communicate better with other people.

The unrestricted and boundless nature of consciousness is mirrored in the unrestricted and boundless nature of the ether or space element, which is associated with the throat chakra. In addition to this, it is associated with the color blue, and the symbol for it is a lotus that is blue and has sixteen petals. When an individual's throat chakra is in a condition of balance, they are better able to connect with and communicate with other people, as well as express themselves in a way that is both crystal clear and full of self-assurance. In addition to this, they are able to pay careful attention to the perspectives of other people and to explain their own needs and feelings in a way that is useful to the situation.

However, when a someone's throat chakra is blocked or out of balance, they may find it difficult to communicate effectively and may also find it difficult to express themselves in a way that is genuine to who they are. This can be a source of frustration for the individual. They might also have a hard time understanding the perspectives of other people and finding the words to express the feelings or requirements that are uniquely their own. Some of the possible physical indicators of an imbalance in the throat chakra include hearing problems, troubles with the neck, shoulders, and jaw, as well as sore throats, thyroid disorders, and neck, shoulder, and jaw pain.

There is a wide variety of practices that can be helpful in bringing the energy of the throat chakra back into balance. These practices can also improve our capacity for clear and effective communication. A range of techniques, like as meditation, yoga, chanting, and breathwork, can be utilized to successfully activate the throat chakra and establish a connection with our own inner voice. These strategies have the ability to help us in expressing ourselves with a higher level of self-assurance and authenticity, as well as in effectively communicating our feelings and requirements to others in a constructive manner.

In addition to these practices, there are a range of other techniques that we may take that have the potential to assist us in enhancing our ability to communicate in a way that is both clear and successful. The following are some of them:

Because it demands one to focus their attention on what is being said by others, active listening is an important skill that is necessary for effective communication. If we really listen to what other people have to say and take what they say to heart, we may be better able to understand the viewpoints of other people and respond in a way that is both productive and compassionate.

Mindfulness in one's utterances Keeping conscious knowledge of one's own words and the manner in which those words affect the people in one's immediate environment is another crucial component of effective communication. If we increase our capacity to connect with other people and to develop meaningful relationships with them by communicating in a way that is both clear and compassionate, we can enhance our ability to connect with other people and to form meaningful relationships with them.

Things like gestures, facial expressions, and body language are examples of forms of non-verbal communication. This type of communication does not include the use of words. When it comes to the effectiveness of a conversation, nonverbal communication can play an incredibly crucial role. We may be able to increase the quality of our communication with others and create stronger ties with those we engage with if we are cognizant of our own nonverbal indicators and if we pay attention to the signs of others around us.

Developing Your Capacity for Empathy As a Closing Remark, Cultivating empathy is one of the most important aspects of effective communication since it allows for better understanding between parties. If we put ourselves in the shoes of the other person and make an effort to fully understand their state of mind as well as their ideas and emotions, we will be able to communicate in a way that is both more empathic and more productive.

To recap, the ability to communicate clearly and effectively with other individuals is highly dependent on the throat chakra's ability to operate in a healthy manner. We may be able to strengthen our capacity to communicate our thoughts and feelings in a way that is both clear and assured, as well as our ability to make meaningful connections with other people, if we are successful in bringing this energy center back into balance and activating it. Adopting practices such as active listening, mindful speech, nonverbal communication, and empathy can help us enhance our ability to communicate clearly and establish more meaningful connections with other people.

The following is an explanation of the meaning and significance of each of the Navatara:

Each of the Navataras, which are found within the Navatara chakra system, carries with it a distinct significance and symbolism of its own. An examination of the meanings and symbolism associated with each of the Navataras is presented in the following order:

1. Janma: The JanmaNavatara is emblematic of birth, new beginnings, and the commencement of a new cycle. It is a representation of a person's potential for self-improvement and development, as well as the accomplishment of the goal they have set for their life. The practice of starting something new and getting things moving is referred to as janma, which is a Sanskrit word that means "transforming force."

2. Sampat The Navatara sign of Sampat is associated with achievement, plenty, and good fortune. The fulfillment of one's material requirements, the upkeep

of one's financial stability, and the increase of money and resources are all represented by this image. Sampat is a symbol of the benefits that accrue as a result of putting in a lot of effort, being dedicated to achieving one's goals, and seeing those goals materialize into reality.

3. Vipat This Navatara relates to challenging periods in one's life as well as challenges, troubles, and trying circumstances. It is a metaphor for the difficulties and struggles that individuals must triumph over in order to develop and advance in their lives. It is vital to display resiliency, flexibility, and the ability to prevail through adversity in order to gain both personal and spiritual development. Only then can one hope to reach their full potential.

4. Kshema The KshemaNavatara is a representation of safety, prosperity, and steadfastness. It is illustrative of a state that is distinguished by contentment, calm, and security. The Kshema is a symbol that stands for the bounties of celestial protection as well as the

capacity to achieve inner peace and harmony in spite of the challenges that life brings. It does this in spite of the fact that life presents its challenges.

5. The Pratyari, also known as the PratyariTheNavatara deity is associated with introspection, transformation, and the cultivation of one's own inner strength. Introspection, self-examination, and the process of coming to terms with oneself, as well as a spiritual awakening, are all appropriate activities during this period. The process of undergoing a personal transformation as well as the building of inner strength and resiliency is referred to as pratyari. This is a term that can be used interchangeably with pratyahara.

6. Sadhaka, you are The SadhakaNavatara is symbolic of self-discipline, commitment, and development in one's relationship with themselves. It is a metaphor for the path to education, growth, and the realization of one's full potential in life. Sadhaka is a term that refers to the significance of self-discipline, concentrated effort, and

constant self-improvement when it comes to achieving one's own personal and spiritual goals.

7. Naidhana (nee: The NaidhanaNavatara describes situations in one's life that put their mettle to the test while also presenting them with opportunity to develop. It is a metaphor for the trials and tribulations that individuals must triumph through in order to develop into more powerful versions of themselves and to grow older. The term naidhana refers to both the karmic lessons and the opportunities for personal growth that are offered to a person as a direct result of being placed in trying circumstances.

8. Mitra: According to Navatar, the sign of Mitra is a symbol of friendship, social connections, and partnerships that are harmonious. It is a metaphor for the importance of creating relationships that are cooperative and helpful, developing a sense of belonging, and establishing meaningful connections with other people. The origin of the name Mitra can be traced back to a Sanskrit word that

describes the positive effects of having harmonious connections as well as the role that friendship plays in the lives of an individual.

Atimitra (9) The Navatara people A representation of compassion, humanitarianism, and selflessness, the atimitra is a Buddhist emblem. It is a symbol of a person's capacity to express love, compassion, and support for other people. The concept of "atimitra" is meant to convey the significance of the importance of being of service to humanity, of engaging in acts of compassion, and of being an example of the characteristics of empathy and selflessness.

CHAKRA REIKI MEDITATION for the Purpose of Healing.

Find a place in your home that is calm and serene where you may go to get some alone time. Your ability to meditate is being hindered by sounds and noises coming from the surrounding surroundings. After putting in the necessary effort, you'll be able to meditate anyplace, even in front of other people if you so choose. Your ability to meditate will not be hindered in the slightest by any disturbances that may take place in the surroundings around you. For the time being, you should choose a tranquil environment in which to practice chakra healing meditation in order to maximize its benefits.

After that, look around until you find a seat that's just right for you. You need to sit in a position in which your legs are crossed and one of your feet is propped up on the other. When one is just getting started, it's feasible that one can find themselves in an awkward position like this. Utilizing cushions can provide you with the support that your knees need. It is essential that there be no tension present in either your limbs or your body at all times. I ask that you gently close your eyes.

(There will be a pause here for ten seconds)

Your back is straight and aligned properly. You should make use of a support if you are unable to keep your spine in a straight position at all times. If you lean against a wall in this manner, you might be able to give your back some support. Kindly keep in mind that you are going to be counted on to continue playing this position for the foreseeable future. It is essential to maintain a posture in which the head is in line with the spine. Your entire physical being should have a sense of calm and composure.

At this moment, bring your attention to the regular pattern of your breathing. It is essential that you do not make any noise at all and that you breathe silently. When you breathe, try not to put too much effort into it. It is important to keep in mind that the process of mending and unblocking your chakras is one that calls for gentleness on your part.

(There will be a ten-second break in the conversation.) You are not in a hurry to get anywhere. You are able to keep a level head under pressure. Your mental state is calm and collected. Your breaths are gentle and calming to listen to. Bring your attention to the feeling of air passing in and out of your nostrils as you breathe. When you breathe, try not to put too much effort into it.

If you take a deep breath in, you should feel a nip in the air that enters your nostrils. It should feel like warm air is exiting from your nostrils whenever you exhale completely. During your practice of deep breathing, you should be aware of the gentle flow of air entering and exiting through your nose. Continue for ten more breaths after that. You have completely lost any credibility at this point.

Understanding the Role of Sensuality in the Process of Spiritual Development and Awakening the Erotic Self

Embracing one's sensuality while simultaneously strengthening one's connection with their senses

Due to the fast-paced and frequently chaotic character of modern life, it is relatively simple for us to get disengaged from the grandeur and depth of our sensory experiences. This can happen for a number of reasons. On the other side, if we consciously engage with our senses, we open ourselves up to a universe in which we have the potential to experience immense joy, profound presence, and the growth of our spirituality. In the following section, we will explore the significance of embracing one's sensuality and provide real examples to assist you in creating a profound connection with your senses. In addition, we will address the importance of embracing one's sensuality.

Exploring our sensory awareness through actively engaging our senses through sight, touch, taste, and smell as well as sound

Our senses are the entryways through which we participate in the world around us and through which we take in information. If we make a concerted effort to examine and engage each of our five senses, the quality of our sensory experiences can be elevated, and our day-to-day lives can take on a new level of presence, both of which are possible results of this endeavor. The following are some exercises that can be used to help you increase your sensory awareness:

Sight: Transform your living space into a calm and lovely sanctuary for the eyes by adorning it with paintings, sculptures, and other works of art, in addition to incorporating elements of nature. This will make your living space seem more at home.

Take some quiet walks outside and allow yourself to become fully involved in the dazzling colors, minute details, and stunning panoramas that are all around you. Engage in some self-reflection while you're out there.

Gazing is a form of meditation in which the practitioner is instructed to direct his or her attention to a particular object or natural scene and then to allow this focus to strengthen the observer's visual sense. This form of meditation can be used to improve one's visual awareness.

Participate in pursuits like gardening, making pottery, or giving yourself a light self-massage in order to get the most out of the tactile sensations that are available to you. Touch: Participate in activities that give you the opportunity to fully feel the sensations of touch.

Feel what it is like to run your fingers over various materials, such as cloth, tree bark, or water, and pay attention to the unique sensations that are generated by each one. For example, fabric has a different texture than tree bark. Learning about the environment through different textures is an enjoyable approach to do it.

Discover the transformational potential of gentle caresses, feather-light touches, and deeper pressure by utilizing a number of different types of touch within the context of your most critical relationships. Specifically, this can help you discover the transformative potential of soft caresses, feather-light touches, and deeper pressure.

Taste: To establish a mindful attitude toward eating, appreciate each mouthful of food while paying attention to the meal's flavors, textures, and scents. This will help you develop a more mindful relationship with eating. You will become more aware of your relationship with food as a result of doing this.

Experiment with a variety of recipes and ingredients so that your taste buds can develop acclimated to a wider variety of flavors and so that you can have a wider variety of gourmet experiences.

Participate in tasting rituals such as wine or chocolate tastings, activities that will allow you to concentrate your attention on the nuances and complexities presented by a variety of flavors. For example, wine tastings and chocolate tastings.

Scent: You may turn your home into a relaxing haven by diffusing essential oils, lighting fragrant candles, or placing fresh cut flowers about the space. Permit yourself to be enveloped by the aromas and allow them to stimulate your senses as they surround you.

Stop what you're doing, both literally and figuratively, and take a deep breath so you can smell the roses. Activate your sense of smell while indulging in the all-natural fragrances of freshly cut grass, aromatic herbs, or coffee that has just been brewed from the bean.

You can utilize scent as a trigger for relaxation and presence in your life if you learn to associate certain aromas with calming activities like meditation or taking a warm bath.

Sound: Experiment with a wide range of musical genres and pay attention to how they alter your state of mind and the emotions you feel as a result of listening to music. Utilize music as a tool to magnify the sensations that you are now experiencing and to conjure up specific locations in your mind.

Spend some time in natural locations where you may listen to the sounds of birds, flowing water, or rustling leaves, and allow the calming or energizing aspects of these sounds to echo inside of you as a result of your time spent there.

Participating in sound healing techniques like chanting, drumming, or utilizing singing bowls, for example, might help you develop a stronger connection with the part of you that lies within. Your hearing will be stimulated and you will experience a greater sense of connection to yourself as a result of participating in these activities.

By consciously connecting with each of your five senses, you can invite a more profound degree of being present, thankfulness, and awareness into your life. These activities will not only enhance the quality of your sensory experiences, but they will also give you access to new avenues for the growth of your spirituality and the investigation of your own inner world.

If the characteristics, behaviors, and ideas that I maintain are accurate reflections of who I am, then they are superior. If they are not accurate representations, then they are not superior. My greatest priority in life is to keep learning about the wonderful things that other people are experts in, regardless of whether or not other people take pleasure in doing so. If no one complements me, not only will I have a negative opinion of myself, but I also won't make the effort to enhance my abilities because I don't feel like I deserve it. If the characteristics, behaviors, and ideas that I maintain are accurate reflections of who I am, then they are superior. If they are not accurate representations, then they are not superior. As a result of the fact that the highest priority in my life is to spend the remainder of it basking in the splendor of other people's areas of expertise, even though I have no plans to better myself in any way, this is the reason.

A Beneficial Instinct (Belief) That Can Assist in the Balancing of the Chakras: On the interior of each one of us.

All of my oddities, habits, and admirable qualities were bestowed upon me by the one who created the cosmos, who is also the one who rules over the entirety of the universe. It is vital that I continue to develop these skills so that I can aid an ever-increasing number of people. My major obligation is to contribute to the wellbeing of the world, so it is imperative that I continue to develop these qualities. As a result of this, I put in a lot of work to develop my specialty, keep up a steady practice of self-analysis at every moment, study quality books, and increase my level of knowledge. Because I am the most perfect creation that God has ever produced, every characteristic, practice, and value that I possess are all gifts from God, who is the ruler of the entire universe. This is due to the fact that I am the most perfect creation that God has ever made.

"Chakra balancing" refers to the process of re-establishing a harmonious flow of energy across the entirety of your body's chakra system. This is the act that is referred to as "chakra balancing."

The consequence of having chakras that are in harmony often translates into a sensation of peace, abundance, relaxation, centeredness, better awareness, and a sense that one loves themselves. When we talk about bringing harmony back to the chakras, there are a few different ways that we may look at what we're talking about. The process by which the energy is brought into a state in which it is harmonious and balanced is one understanding of what it means to balance the chakras, and this interpretation is quite popular.

To restore a chakra's equilibrium, all that is necessary is to treat its individual components in the event that any of those components have become imbalanced or blocked. Each chakra is an independent part of a system that functions as a whole. You are aware that each chakra has its own unique relationship with the others, and that these relationships are perfectly integrated now that you understand how the chakras work, therefore you are aware that these ties are seamless. As a consequence of this, it is vital, when attempting to balance the chakras, to take into mind each chakra, the centers that are close to it, as well as the energy that travels throughout the entire system as a whole.

The preservation of a balanced stream, which in turn will encourage the movement of energy throughout the body, can be contributed to by the balancing of the chakras, which contributes to the maintenance of a balanced stream. The multiple sources of tension and obligations that are experienced in day-to-day life are the root cause of the moment-to-moment shifts in the flow of energy that take place. These exchanges may leave you feeling tired, satisfied, or supported, depending on how you choose to respond to them. Encounters from the past, particularly those that were not effectively dealt with, often leave a lasting impression on how you feel, which in turn influences the flow of your energy in the here and now. In particular, those encounters that were not well dealt with are likely to have this effect.

The following is a selection of the several advantages that can be gained as a consequence of obtaining chakra balance:

Helps to release any and all emotional energy, as well as habits that have become blocked

Provides you with the capacity to enter higher realms of awareness at any time you choose to do so.

You will be able to experience energetic frequencies that will assist you in recognizing when an energy flow is not serving you well. This will enable you to transition to a higher frequency that will keep you aligned to your energy. You will be able to do this because you will be able to detect when an energy flow is not serving you well.

When all of a person's chakras are functioning properly, that person may find that they are completely devoid of emotional experience. Visions of images and colors, feelings of being nurtured and supported, sensations of energy moving inside them, feelings of being nurtured and supported, visions of images and colors, or even a state of deep relaxation could be experienced by other people. Some people may experience intense emotional releases, such as uncontrollable sobbing, while others may get considerable insight into certain aspects of their lives. Some people may have both of these experiences. Everyone has an own perspective on how they felt about it. But once your chakras are balanced, or once you at least know how to perceive when one of them is out of balance and can seek to bring it back to harmony, your life will change for the better permanently, and it will change for the better forever. This is because once your chakras are balanced, you will know how to recognize when one of them is out of balance and will be able to bring it back to equilibrium.

Meditation Is Necessary Before Healing the Chakras

Before beginning your journey to heal your chakras, it is essential for you to ensure that all of the necessary preparations have been made, as this will allow the healing process to go as smoothly as possible. In order to get you started with chakra healing, this chapter will take you step-by-step through the most important parts of the preparation process. If you take the time to prepare yourself intellectually, emotionally, and physically before beginning the process, you will be able to create an atmosphere that is conducive to profound healing and transformation. This will allow you to create an environment that is conducive to profound healing and transformation. In order to be prepared for chakra healing, let's have a look at some of the most essential components.

The significance of education and the ability to comprehend:

In order to get yourself prepared for chakra healing, the first thing you need to do is educate yourself about the chakra system and have a solid understanding of it. Only then can you begin to prepare yourself for the healing process. Gain an understanding of the seven basic chakras, including their positions, the qualities that are associated with them, and the roles that they play in the body. Acquire a grasp of the ways in which the seven major chakras influence your physical well-being, as well as the manner in which they affect your emotional well-being and your spiritual well-being. If you have this understanding, you will be able to spot chakra imbalances and work with each chakra in an efficient manner. This knowledge will offer you a foundation for your journey toward chakra healing.

Setting Your Intentions: Before beginning chakra healing, one of the most important things you can do is to carefully consider and articulate your goals and objectives for the process. Spend some time thinking on what it is that you want to achieve via the process of chakra healing and the goals that you have set for yourself. Do you wish to improve your emotional well-being, deepen your spiritual connection, establish emotional equilibrium, or broaden your personal horizons? First, you should create a clear statement of your objectives, and then you should write them down. During the course of the healing process, your goals will serve as a map and a compass, directing your energy and concentration in the right direction. Developing a Sacred

Environment: It is essential that you create a space that is totally committed to and sacred for the purpose of your chakra healing practice. You should choose an area in your house that is quiet and peaceful so that you can carry out the self-healing practices you've chosen without being disturbed. First get rid of any clutter, and then rearrange the furniture in such a way that it makes you feel relaxed and tranquil. Consider including elements into the space that have a powerful energetic resonance with each chakra, such as stones, essential oils, candles, or symbolic representations of these things. This sacred location will act as a haven for the healing of your chakras, providing an environment that is amenable to engaging in introspective activities to a greater degree.

Getting Grounded and Centered: In order to prepare yourself for chakra healing, it is necessary to engage in activities that will help you get grounded and centered. When you practice grounding, you connect yourself with the energy of the earth, which in turn provides you with a feeling of support and stability. The process of centering helps you realign your energy and bring your attention within, so that you can reap the benefits of both. You should participate in activities that help you feel more anchored and centered, such as going barefoot for a walk in the woods, building a mindfulness practice, or indulging in deep breathing exercises. These kinds of activities will help you feel more grounded and focused. These practices help to relax the mind, put your energy back into balance, and establish a solid foundation for the restoration of your chakras.

Affirmations that stimulate and fortify one's connection to one's heart chakra

In this chapter, you will be given some very powerful affirmations with the intention of supporting you in opening up and harmonizing the space surrounding your Heart. Affirmations with a focus on the heart chakra will help you transform your thinking and energy to a more loving and compassionate place. This can be accomplished through practicing these affirmations regularly. Affirmations, when repeated with the aim of stimulating and harmonizing the energy of the Heart center, can play a vital part in the process of rewriting the patterns that are stored in our subconcious minds and sending healing vibrations to this energy center. This can be accomplished by repeating the affirmations with the intention of energizing and harmonizing the energy of the Heart center.

It is important to keep in mind that both our ideas and our words contain energy, and that this energy has the potential to have an effect in the physical world. When you first become aware of the power of your words, you won't be able to control what you say, neither to yourself nor to other people, and this will be the case regardless of whether you are speaking to yourself or to others. You won't allow yourself think anything, whether it be about yourself or about other people, when you first become aware of the power of your ideas. This is true whether you are thinking about yourself or about other people. Changing your thoughts and beliefs so that they are more in line with who you truly are can be made easier if you work with the affirmations that are provided below on a consistent basis. This will address any blockages that have formed in the Heart space and direct healing energy to the center of your Heart.

"Just as the spirit takes on the qualities of the things that we think about, so does the body take on the qualities of what we eat."

— A Kémitic Proverb From an Ancient Time Period

As we discovered in our earlier discussions on the first three chakras, affirmations are most effective when they are repeated on a regular basis in order to fully realize their potential. Repeating these powerful affirmations on a regular basis can make a major impact in how quickly you recover from whatever ails you. It is essential, however, that you have a powerful desire and that you honestly believe the words that you are saying in order for them to be effective. You should make an effort to internalize the affirmations and focus on developing a connection with the energy that is evoked by the statements and the phrases. Do everything in your power to internalize the affirmations.

You can say the following affirmations out loud, in front of a mirror (remembering to look yourself in the eye as you do so), write them down, or repeat them to yourself at certain moments throughout the day (when you're standing in line, on your commute to and from work, when you get up/before bed, etc.). You can also look yourself in the eye while you do any of these things. While you are doing this, you can additionally look yourself in the eye. You may wish to select one or more of these affirmations as your aim for the day, or you may decide to meditate on one or more of these statements. Either way, you have options. You can use a single affirmation or a mix of them whenever you set a goal, whether it is before a heart-opening yoga practice or before you use a crystal or essential oil to heal the Heart region. Whenever you establish a goal, you have the option of using either a single affirmation or a combination of them. whatever it is that you consider to be the most significant at that particular instant in time.

It is possible for you to select one Heart chakra affirmation that speaks to you the most and to maintain a constant focus on this affirmation for a period of time before moving on to another. You can do this by choosing the affirmation that speaks to you the most and clicking here. You might also try to find a way to connect with the following affirmations by reading them every day and allocating some time in your schedule to do so. It can be done in any way you like; there is no right or wrong way to do it!

I am able to give and take love without making an effort and without attaching any conditions to either experience.

My unalienable right to love and be loved in return cannot be taken away from me.

It is safe for me to lower my defenses and open up the potential of romantic attachment in my heart.

I am courageous enough to listen to and respect what my heart has to say about a situation.

I am someone who is worthy of the most profound love, and I am also someone who can easily love other people.

Compassion encompasses not only myself but also the people in my immediate environment.

I am able to cultivate compassionate and supportive relationships, not only with myself but also with other people.

I have compassion for my heart, my soul, and my spirit, and I give love and light to these parts of myself. I am okay with myself.

My emotional center is open and airy, and it reverberates with the vitality of emerald-colored light.

My life is one that is in balance with people who are close to me as well as in harmony with all other beings in the universe.

There is no cap on the amount of love that one can show to another person.

My emotions have recovered from the hurt they experienced in the past.

I have made the choice to let go of any and all animosity I may have harbored.

My natural, or default, state of being is one that is exemplified by love and concern for others.

Techniques for Correct Pronunciation as Well as Chanting

The practice of Mantra Yoga places a strong emphasis on correct pronunciation as well as chanting techniques. The power of mantras lies in correctly pronouncing them and chanting them in a rhythmic manner because mantras are holy sound vibrations. Mantras have the potential to significantly increase their transformative power if they are recited with the proper articulation of each word and the appropriate modulation of voice. In this comprehensive book, we will investigate the importance of correct pronunciation, the methods for achieving mastery of pronunciation, and the expertise required for effective chanting when performing mantra meditation.

The Importance of Being Able to Pronounce Things Correctly
In the practice of Mantra Yoga, it is believed that each syllable of a mantra

possesses its own unique vibrational frequency and resonance. The correct pronunciation guarantees that these vibrations are formed appropriately, which has a deeper influence on the subtle energy system of the practitioner. The following are some of the reasons why correct pronunciation is so important:

Correct pronunciation of the mantra links the energy of the practitioner with the inherent power of the mantra, creating a synergistic connection between the person and the sacred sound.

Intentions are effectively channeled through the correct pronounciation of mantras, which are used in yoga and other forms of meditation. When words are spoken mindfully, the vibrational energy of those words coincides with the choices being made, which strengthens concentration and increases the efficiency of the exercise.

Sacred languages such as Sanskrit have been passed down through the centuries with painstaking attention paid to their pronunciation in order to preserve the traditions associated with them. The correct pronunciation shows respect for the family lineage and ensures the preservation of time-honored rituals.

The correct pronounciation is an act of respect for the cultural and linguistic history of the holy language. This acknowledges the value of the language as a medium for spiritual insight and sacred expression.

Accurate pronounciation heightens the spiritual experience of the practitioner, creating a sense of reverence and a bond with the divine. This results in an ascent in one's spiritual status.

Using Chakras to Manifest Your Desires and Improve Your Relationships

Utilizing the power of our thoughts and intentions, the process of manifesting our wants is the act of bringing them closer to becoming a reality. Because we now have a better grasp of the relationship between the chakras and the process of manifestation, we are able to make better use of the chakras to enhance our ability to bring our wishes closer to becoming a reality.

Using Healing of the Chakras to Bring About Manifestation

Healing of the chakras can be an extremely effective method of manifestation. We are able to clear energy blockages and connect our vibration with the goals we wish to manifest if we put in the effort to bring each chakra into balance and to awaken it. Visualizing each chakra as a spinning wheel of energy and imagining it spreading positive energy throughout our body is one technique to employ chakra healing for manifestation. Another way is to image each chakra as a spinning wheel of energy. Utilizing crystals or other forms of energy instruments that are related with each chakra is yet another method of applying chakra healing to the process of manifestation. By way of illustration, making use of a red jasper crystal can assist in balancing and activating the root chakra, whereas making use of a citrine crystal can assist in balancing and activating the solar plexus chakra.

The Integration of Chakra Healing into the Practice of Manifestation

When we incorporate chakra healing into our manifestation practice, it can assist to strengthen our ability to bring our goals into reality and make the process go more swiftly. Having distinct intentions for each chakra can be an effective means of incorporating chakra healing into our practice of manifesting our desires. Take, for instance, the scenario in which we desire to bring greater abundance into our lives. In that situation, we can decide to make it our goal to bring our solar plexus chakra, which is connected to feelings of personal power and abundance, into a state of balance and activation.

Your Soul and the Way You Get to Work in the Morning

Everyone has had the unfortunate experience of being stuck in a mile-long line of traffic that seemingly materialized out of nowhere. Many of us are guilty of mumbling profanities under our breath, forcefully laying on the car horn, or blaming the "idiot" driver up ahead who is generating the unreasonably lengthy line of traffic. We do all of these things because we are frustrated by the excessively long line of traffic. What we frequently forget to take into account, though, is the possibility that the traffic is the consequence of a terrible vehicle accident. When we are in situations like this and neglect to examine the options, we limit the energy that is available to our hearts. The circumstance is not approached with acceptance, compassion, love, or open-mindedness on our part. We allow the vitality of our Heart to get constrained by our disappointments, and we allow a momentary loss of our sense of calmness to occur as a result. If you feel that you are getting more and more irritated while you are sitting in traffic, then you should attempt the following exercise the next time it happens to you:

Purification of the Breath

While you wait in traffic, take a few calm breaths in and out.

Imagine that as you take a deep breath in, your lungs are being filled with peace, acceptance, and compassion.

Imagine that when you let out your breath, your body is letting go of all of the unpleasant feelings that your current circumstance is causing you to experience, such as anger, impatience, and aggravation.

Positions of Meditation

Assume a seated position with your legs put in front of you as you perform Navasana, also known as the boat pose.

Bring your knees up to your chest and hold them there. After that, prop up the posterior aspect of your knees with a support so that you may lift your feet off the ground and maintain your balance while seated on your ischium.

Be sure to keep your shoulders pulled back and your chest up while you do this. It is imperative that the weight be spread forward, toward the front of the ischium, while simultaneously drawing the navel in toward the spine. Your core muscles will be strengthened as a result of your doing this activity.

While doing so, stretch your arms forward and raise your legs as high as you can.

As you exhale, bring your upper arms around to your front and clasp your hands together. Then, slowly lower your lower extremities until they are almost touching the floor, but be careful that they do not fully touch the floor. Bring your feet down to a position where they are only a few centimeters off the ground.

Next, take a deep breath in. While you are doing this, gradually return to the position of the boat.

Continue performing this up to a maximum of five times.

Following that, you are free to recline on your back.

Visualize the color yellow erupting from your solar plexus chakra as you go through this practice. After that, repeat the word "Ram" aloud.

When you hold this role, you are altering the area of your life that is responsible for determining your level of productivity and your sense of self-worth. Fear and a lack of forward movement will be less likely to occur as a result of this.

The word "chakra" comes from an old Sanskrit word that means "wheel," and it describes the activity that occurs at the various energy centers that are dispersed throughout the body. This practice has also been referred to as energy medicine or energetic therapy, and it is founded on the spiritual teachings of ancient civilizations from India, China, and Japan.

The traditional practitioners of medicine and healing in these regions were aware of something referred to as the subtle body, which can be defined as the energy that circulates throughout and around our bodies, is drawn to particular regions, and ensures that our organs work as they should. In Chinese medicine, the paths that this energy travels are referred to as meridians, and both acupuncture and Chinese herbal therapy, which are both alternative forms of treatment, depend on it.

These meridians are responsible for transporting energy from one part of the body to another, physically passing over hundreds of chakra points (which are typically located close to or directly above glands, nerve clusters, and important organs). However, there are seven locations spread throughout the body that bring together all of these meridians to form the major chakras. These are the chakras that are responsible for the overall regulation of the body, not just specific parts.

These primary energy centers are responsible for actively and passively absorbing energy from our surrounding environment. Not only do they get their vitality from the sun, from the fresh air, and from the natural cycles of night and day, but they also get their energy from the food that we eat and from the habits and routines that we have. If we are healthy, then the energy in our meridians and chakras moves smoothly and we maintain a sense of wellness throughout the day. As in the case of the pulmonary blood systems, their normal state is to be one in which they are rotating, churning, recycling, and replenishing the energy.

For a variety of reasons, which we shall elaborate on in the following section, people have long held the belief that specific chakras are responsible for regulating different emotional patterns and states of being as well. In practice, you can make a beneficial and immediate impact on your self-confidence, physical health, and professional accomplishments by bringing your chakras into balance.

THE STATE THAT EACH OF THE CHAKRAS ARE IN

Comparing the chakras to the tires on your automobile is the most straightforward method for gaining an understanding of the state that the chakras need to be in for them to function effectively.

For optimal performance, a tire needs to be inflated to a predetermined pressure. It is necessary to inflate it to the correct level.

Tires that are under- or over-inflated can cause a number of difficulties, including a loss of traction, reduced stopping power, decreased longevity, increased fuel consumption, the possibility of tire rupture, and notably premature wear on the tire.

A tire that is properly inflated will wear more evenly and will last longer.

It is the same way with the chakras; the only difference is that we do not use the word "inflate" but rather the word "balance" to refer to what is, in essence, the same thing.

If a chakra is either too "inflated" or not "inflated" enough, there will be issues with its ability to cling to life; yet, if it is "inflated" enough, it will adhere correctly.

Each chakra serves a unique purpose, and in order for the body to function properly, all of the chakras need to be in alignment with one another because they are interconnected. An imbalance in one chakra automatically results in an imbalance in the others, just as the stability of a vehicle is dependent on the effective operation of all of its tires.

The following are some of the most important roles that the chakras play:

1st chakra, sometimes known as the root chakra: safety

The second chakra, often known as the sacred chakra of vitality

The third chakra, sometimes known as the solar plexus chakra, governs personality.

Love resides in the fourth chakra, the heart chakra.

The fifth chakra, sometimes known as the throat chakra, is associated with communication.

The sixth chakra and the third eye chakra:

7th chakra awareness, coronal chakra: familiarity

If any of these chakras are out of alignment, the energy that they are supposed to channel will either become excessive or inadequate. Therefore, feelings of dread can be brought on by insufficient activity in the first chakra, whilst feelings of overconfidence can be brought on by excessive activity in the first chakra. To keep a body in good health, in shape, and in agreement with the world, it is necessary that all of these chakras work in a balanced way, and if they want to take you away, you have to take care of them the same way you would take care of the tires on your car. This creates a situation in which there is poor adaptation to life.

Aromatherapy as a Means of Restoring Chakra Balance

Essential oils are not much more than the aromatic essences of plants that have been extracted, and their purpose is to assist balance, heal, and purify the chakras so that radiant energy can flow. When it comes to aromatherapy, certain essential oils will result in results that are comparable to those of color therapy.

Every variety of essential oil will generate its own unique energy pattern, which will then resonate on a slightly varied range of frequencies. The energy patterns that are produced by their vibrations will always have some kind of connection to the energy patterns that are produced by your seven primary chakras. Re-aligning the vibrations of your energy patterns can also be accomplished with the help of the pure resonance of the oils.

The following is a list of essential oils, along with the chakras that each one stimulates:

Jasmine, rose, tangerine, cinnamon, and Melissa are all associated with the sacral chakra.

Rosemary, peppermint, juniper, black pepper, sandalwood, and lavender are the essential oils associated with the navel chakra.

Cardamom, ginger, patchouli, rosewood sage, and other spices represent the root chakra.

Vanilla, neroli, Melissa, geranium, chamomile, bergamot, and many other essential oils are associated with the heart chakra.

Sage, rose, oregano, pine, thyme, cedar, and basil are the essential oils associated with the third eye chakra.

Cypress, lavender, Roman chamomile, and German chamomile are all associated with the throat chakra.

Asanas for Restoring Harmony to the Heart Chakra in Yoga

The following yoga positions will assist you in stimulating and opening your heart chakra if you practice them regularly:

Ustrasana, often known as the Camel Pose

Put yourself in a position where you are on your knees. Check that the distance between your knees is roughly equal to the distance between your hips.

Put your heels up and sit back.

The next step is to place your hands in a position where they are resting on your chest.

Put your toes together.

Raise yourself up so that your thighs are parallel to the floor and your hips are directly over your knees.

Place your palms on the lower half of your back in this position. Check that the tips of your fingers are pointing in an upward direction. While you are doing this, bring your sacrum down toward the floor, and at the same time, elevate the frontal hip bones up toward the ceiling.

Lean backwards while tilting your head and putting your neck in a hyperextended position. Put your hands on your heels and feel them. Before you arch your back, focus your thoughts on something or someone that you love. Give that person or thing your full attention during this movement.

Keep your body in that position while you breathe in a calm and collected manner.

Imagine that a bright green light is emanating from within your heart chakra while you continue to do this.

Repeat the word "Yam" again and over.

After taking a few slow, deep breaths, readjust the position of your head in relation to your sacrum. Place your weight on your heels. You can return your hands to their previous position by bringing them together and placing them on your chest. Make a low bow to me.

Whenever you strike this stance, you are having an effect on the region of your life that is responsible for governing love. You will be able to repair any previous emotional wounds and feel more open to love after practicing the camel stance.

Bhujangasana, also known as the Cobra Pose

First, assume the prone posture by lying on your back and bringing your elbows to the ground in front of you. Your hands should be stretched out in front of you while you keep your feet together.

Now take a deep breath in and lift your upper body upward while keeping your hands in this position. While doing so, shift your focus upward and lengthen the back of your neck.

In the beginning, students may choose to concentrate on perfecting the half cobra stance. The full cobra stance, often known as the advanced version, is a little bit different.

As you lie on your stomach in the prone position, place your hands on the floor with your elbows bent. Your hands need to be positioned such that they are next to your chest.

Always remember to keep your legs connected together and extended. It is important to keep your pubis, feet, and thighs pressed firmly against the floor.

Take a long, slow breath in, and as you do so, bring your chest up toward the ceiling while pressing your palms firmly onto the floor. Maintain a backward tilt in your shoulders, an upward stare, and a lengthened neck by pressing your shoulders backward. Your belly button, also known as your navel, ought to be on the ground.

Maintain this position for at least five breaths throughout the duration of the exercise. After that, let your breath out and return slowly to the starting position. Try holding the stance for an additional two or three times.

"Ajna" The area known as the Third Eye The Chakra is located in the middle of the forehead.

"Descending triangle within a circle" is the symbol.

The Ajna serves as the primary command post. Indigo is the hue that is connected with this point, which may be found in the space between the eyebrows. There are others who refer to it as their "third eye." This Chakra is concerned with the various ideas and emotions that are experienced by an individual. This encompasses their level of wisdom and intelligence, as well as their level of detachment and insight, understanding in, and reasoning. When this chakra is out of alignment, a variety of different physical characteristics might start to manifest in the body. Eyestrain, difficulties learning, panic attacks, seizures, spinal dysfunction, fear of the truth, inability to concentrate, migraines, and nightmares are all included in this category of symptoms. It is possible to have a new reality as well as improved concentration and focus when one's chakras are in a state of equilibrium. Both mint and jasmine are helpful for balancing this chakra.

The Ajna Chakra, often known as the third eye, is the source of a variety of issues, including problems with the eyes, an inability to visualize things well, and a poor memory. It is possible for a person to suffer from persistent headaches and even persistent nightmares as a result of being exposed to it on a regular basis. Those who are lacking in this particular chakra are more likely to have hallucinations and bad dreams than those who have plenty of it.

The third eye chakra is located in the space between your eyes, and it is responsible for the regulation of your neurological systems, as well as your brain, pineal glands, pituitary gland, and ears, nose, and eyes. Your trust, intuition, and ability to coordinate with others are all directly impacted by the chakra. Your trust, intuition, and ability to coordinate are all going to be directly impacted as a result of this.

If you have an imbalance in this chakra, you may have problems with self-discipline, sleep disorders, notions of judgment and reality, emotional intelligence, disorientation, blindness, stroke, seizures, brain tumors, arrogance, pride, learning impairments, and sleep disorders. You also may have issues with emotional intelligence and emotional intelligence.

The third eye chakra provides you with the ability to gain perspective on a situation and is essential to both learning and wisdom. Your intuitive intelligence and connection to the cosmic awareness are both associated with this chakra. You are able to distinguish between reality and fantasy with the assistance of your third eye chakra. If there is a blockage in the flow of energy via this chakra, you may experience feelings of mistrust as well as self-doubt. You are able to connect with the knowledge that resides within you and receive direction regarding the decisions that you make when your chakras are open and unblocked.

Bringing the Chakras into Harmony Through Complementary and Alternative Healing Methods and Other Practices

The purpose of chakra balancing is to facilitate a steady flow in order to maintain our overall energy level. We have a habit of engaging in a great number of activities throughout the day that frequently result in an excessive amount of stress and lead to shifts in our energy levels by the end of the day. Some of these hobbies may provide a sense of fulfillment and benefit, while others may be exceedingly taxing on one's energy levels. Previous experiences and occurrences frequently leave a long-lasting impression on our feelings, which in turn influences how we make use of our energy on a day-to-day basis.

The interruption and alterations in the flow of our energy, which create chakra imbalances, are the root cause of stress in our bodies. When the chakras are out of harmony, it can have an effect on the amount of energy that is moving through our bodies. When there is a restriction on the free flow of energy, it is insufficient. On the other side, it is said to be hyperactive when there is an abnormally large increase in the flow of energy that is not being controlled. When there is an imbalance in the amount of consistent flow of energy, balancing it out is necessary, as is the regulation of it when it becomes excessive.

When it comes to the methods that can be used to bring our chakras back into alignment, they can be divided into three categories: those that include the transfer of energy from within ourselves or from another person, those that involve an introspective or contemplative practice, and those that are focused on physical activity.

Bringing more harmony to your chakras can be accomplished in a variety of ways throughout the day, including the following:

Chakra yoga refers to the practice of opening, cleansing, and balancing the energy centers, also known as chakras, located throughout our bodies by employing controlled breathing (pranayama) and various yoga postures. By practicing chakra yoga, we can achieve optimal health and operate to the extent of our full potential. This is because the yoga helps our energy centers remain balanced and open.

Hatha yoga postures are typically practiced because they strive to keep our body straight or aligned, particularly the spine. This is one of the primary reasons why these postures are favored. The spine acts as the gatekeeper for the flow of energy through the chakras.

The Link to the Cosmic Realm

When you are seated and attempting to build a connection between your creative energy and the outside world, you are frequently channeling through your chakras, whether or not you are aware of this fact. Visualization is a process that may be described as what happens when someone is by themselves and thinks about something they are working toward obtaining. While you are in this position, you are seated and you are asking the divine design of the universe as well as the energy of the universe to assist you in materializing the specific concept that you are attempting to bring into existence. Because of this, you need to be aware that when you sit down and channel your focus and your intention, you need the energy from the cosmos in order to be able to bring the concept into manifestation. This is something that you must be aware of.

It is thought that 35 000 years ago, one being with infinite power and wisdom created the cosmos, and with that creation, everything was set into motion. This belief dates back to the beginning of recorded history. At that precise instant, the physical manifestations of everything that ever had been and all that will ever be were created. A person is seeking that potential energy from the universe when they sit down and focus their energies on attempting to achieve their life plans as well as trying to focus on the intent they are trying to generate. This is because when a person does this, they are asking the universe for that energy. After that, the energy is carried into the body through the chakras, which act as either a conductor or a superhighway. The energy is able to connect all the way through you, and it is able to become manifest based on all of the energies, as well as the connecting and alignment of all of the factors along the spine and that are made along the process to ensure that you are able to align the outcome of the universe into real and meaningful action.

You are able to plug in and receive the messages that are flowing from the divine cosmos because the universe is able to channel this information to your chakras and is able to assist you in doing so. Without these connections, much like a person who is lost in the dark without a map, we wander around looking for whatever it is that we are out of sync with and hoping to achieve completeness from the source of that dissonance. When we are hungry, we eat too much, which leads to weight gain;

when we are longing for love, we overindulge in sexual activity.

All things in moderation are beneficial to the body; however, when we become out of alignment, just as a mobile phone's battery will die if it isn't charged, so too will a person run out of steam as well as the energy to be able to move forward with their cause if they do not have the appropriate amount of connection and alignment with the appropriate sources.

When you are trying to get a clear signal, it is necessary to take the time and to root yourself firmly in the present so that you will be able to connect and will be able to find your way through the static. Think of yourself as a radio antenna that is trying to connect through all of the static and the white noise of the beyond. When you are trying to get a clear signal, it is necessary to take the time and to root yourself firmly in the present. And there is a lot of static these days, now more than ever, what with social media and continual television coverage, both of which are always broadcasting the same terrible news on a daily basis 24 hours a day, seven days a week throughout the year. You will, in every circumstance, find that you are looking for a way to reconnect, but you will have a very difficult time doing so owing to the fact that you are unable to get past the static while you are trying to locate that connection.

We are going to investigate different ways that you will be able to reconnect yourself and find that balance so that you will be able to keep your chakras aligned. Additionally, you are going to learn how to plug into the energy of the universe without having to worry about falling out of sync and out of tune with the rest of the universe because you will be able to learn how to plug into the energy of the universe. There are a lot of different ways that you may tune in and get ready for the different distractions that you can run into on a daily basis. One of these methods is through practicing mindfulness. You need to have a firm grasp on what is real and what is not, what constitutes a priority and what does not, and how to properly identify and prioritize the various aspects of your life. The state of your physical health and the health of others who are traveling with you should be your primary concern.

Instructions to Help You Get Started Practicing Belly Breathing

To begin, take a deep breath in and try to bring it all the way down into your belly. Observe the expansion of your stomach in order to sharpen your focus. Additionally, you can direct your attention on the hands that you had placed on the belly rise earlier. It is not necessary for you to place your hands in your belly if you continue practicing, but if you find that the exercise is more enjoyable with your hands there, feel free to keep them there.

Make sure that you are keeping your breath in your belly when you exhale and your hands and belly move downwards towards your spine; this indicates that you are holding your breath there. Avoid letting your prana leave your body and instead focus on drawing the vital energy into your being.

pretend that you are stocking a store with each breath that you inhale, and then pretend that you are expelling while keeping the breath that is still in your abdomen. This will enable you to quickly fill your stomach with air and will assist you in doing so more quickly.

And these are all of the stages that are necessary for you to learn in order to properly perform the belly breathing techniques. Always make sure that you have completed at least 10 breaths in order to properly recuperate. If you are used to the shallow breaths of yoga, switching to belly breathing could be difficult at first because you are accustomed to taking in a smaller volume of oxygen. You can just give your normal breathing pattern a try and work on practicing belly breathing as the days go by.

You should make it a point to practice belly breathing at least once or twice a day, but especially when you feel like both your body and mind are dragging. You will notice a change in yourself as well as an increase in your overall energy levels as a result of this activity.

Journal Prompts to Use During the Process of Healing Through Shadow Work

The following questions for your diary are designed to aid you in deciding the parts of your life that require attention and effort on your part, and they are supplied for this purpose. You will begin to get insight into the elements that contribute to your pain as well as the techniques by which you could overcome it if you go deeper into these concerns. So, tell me, are you prepared to face this challenge?

Which significant lessons about living a meaningful life can I garner from the things I've done in the past?

How do I currently counteract the negative thoughts and sensations that I experience? What are some of the methods that I do this? Are these ways of dealing with stress conducive to a healthy lifestyle?

Which of these situations, relationships, or examinations are I willing to give up? If I keep focusing my attention on these upsetting ideas, memories, or energy, what are the repercussions that this will have for my day-to-day life?

What kind of reaction am I supposed to have when the behaviors of other people make me feel badly? Why do the things that trigger my emotional reactions have such a significant influence on me, and what are some of the things that set them off?

How can I protect myself against the thoughts, emotions, and situations that tend to bring out the worst in me, and what are they? Do I frequently form opinions about other individuals based on certain qualities or behaviors that I observe in them?

How can I reign in my irrational sentiments of rage? What steps can I take to increase my ability to deal with this issue, and what strategies are available to me?

How can I accept the truth that I am susceptible to being hurt? Do I make an effort to cover it up or try to hide it, or am I able to recognize it and accept it for what it is?

Which aspects of myself do I find it difficult to accept, and which aspects do I actively dislike? Why?

What are some ways that I can be more loving and compassionate to myself? How might I go about accomplishing this goal?

Which of my previous experiences am I allowed to feel embarrassed about? Is there anything I did in the past that I look back on with deep regret, and if so, what was it?

When I was a kid, did I ever get the impression that I was the only one in the room or that I was being overlooked by adults? Do the things I figured out as a result of this event still relate to how I live my life now? How?

Have there been occasions in which I have fallen short of meeting the expectations of another person? I want to make atonement and heal the relationships that were damaged; is it really possible?

Do I frequently try to impose my will on the decisions or actions of other people? What are some strategies I may use to gain the upper hand and gain influence over them?

Is there anyone in my life who I haven't really forgiven yet, and if so, who is it that I need to apologize to? Why? Do you believe it's OK for me to forgive them at this point?

Where exactly do my personal boundaries reside, and what can I do to improve my ability to re-establish them when they've been breached?

You are more than welcome to ponder on the questions posed and the answers given here while you are engaging in the process of healing and integrating.

www.ingramcontent.com/pod-product-compliance
Lightning Source LLC
Chambersburg PA
CBHW052131110526
44591CB00012B/1682